THE PETITATION COMPANION

Enhance the lives of you and your pets with Mindfulness Meditation

Elisabeth Paige, DrPH & Joanne Leslie

The Petitation Companion
Copyright © 2016 by Elisabeth Paige

All rights reserved. No part of this book may be reproduced or transmitted in any form or by any means without written permission from the author.

Printed in USA

DEDICATION

It took so many beings to create this book: some had two legs, some four. Each spoke a language that was different, but, somehow, we communicated and we learned from each other.

Some of the names were unique to the four-legged variety: the canines—Wesley and Willie and Pago and Pippi and Mikey with the fuzzy face that we miss so much. The feline that we miss the most was our Wolfie. They offered the inspiration.

Others offered the support: my father Fred, always there for all of us. Your humor and critique, your ever-present crooked smile has been our reason. Cousin Steve of On Track Productions, you have made everything sound so wonderful.

My sister Stephanie, my opposite—and we all need one of those.

My partner Kim—it would take a book to tell you about her.

Jill and Damian, Colleen and Darlene, Anne and Beth (I miss you every day.), thank you for keeping the machinery oiled.

Thanks to my ever-present friend Lisa and a special thank you to her brother, A. Ching, who photographed Pago and Pippi.

To Joanne, my mother and creative partner—amazing. We've been working together since I could barely speak, and we haven't killed each other yet. This project has been fun, and we can't wait to continue with the ones we've already begun.

We lost Pago after he waged a brave 15-month battle with cancer. He was very special and we miss him terribly.

With everything that's going on, we all may need to meditate.

practice mindfulness meditation with your pets

To stream your free copies of the Petitations, after you have purchased the book, go to page 149 and follow the instructions.

Enhance the lives of you and your pets
with Mindfulness Meditation

THE PETITATION COMPANION

CONTENTS

	The Introduction	7
I.	The Petting Petitation & Pet Scan	22
II.	The Wisdom Petitation	47
III.	The Walking Petitation	57
IV.	The Equanimity Petitation	78
V.	The Loving Kindness Petitation	88
VI.	The Self Compassion Petitation	99
VII.	The Appreciative Joy Petitation	110
VIII.	The Grief Petitation	120
IX.	The Gratitude Petitation	128
X.	Too Close to Our Hearts	140
XI.	Review of Petitation Practices	147

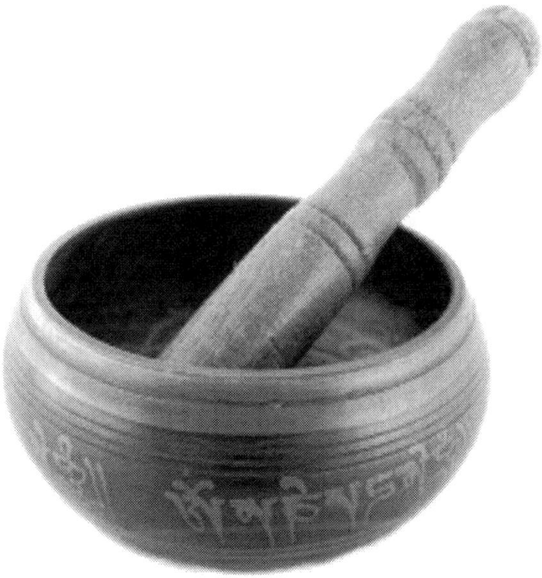

Enhance the lives of you and your pets with Mindfulness Meditation

THE PETITATION COMPANION

What are Petitations? After we've spent some time together, you'll not only know what Petitations are, but you'll be enjoying your meditating, and you and your pets will have more fun than you ever thought possible.

I know you can have fun while you meditate. How would you like to try meditation with me, a geeky, scientifically minded, quasi-Buddhist dog? That's exactly what's in store for you when you accompany me on this ride throughout The Petitation Companion.

One day, about five years ago, Mom said to no one in particular, "I am going to try to meditate for about ten minutes. I'll let you in when I'm done."

Then she went into her bedroom and shut the door in my face. Soft, soothing music floated from Mom's room, as I whined and barked and refused to stop. After what seemed like hours, she finally let me in. She looked so annoyed.

How strange. She rarely got angry at me, but I couldn't think of anything I had done wrong. Mom sat back on the bed. I had destroyed all her pillows and twisted up the bed spread so I knew it would take her forever to figure out where everything belonged, but doing it was so much fun.

Her eyes were closed and it looked like something was horribly wrong. Why was she so mad at me?

She was clenching her jaw and scrunching up her forehead. I didn't even know if she knew I was there. I jumped into her lap and licked her face.

Mom sighed. "I've been trying to meditate. My doctor says I should quiet my mind and try to focus my attention on my breath. It's so frustrating—my mind is all over the place. First, it's on laundry— the mountain of awfully dirty, smelly clothes in the bedroom. Next, it's what to cook for dinner, and the shopping I still have to do. Then it's the episode of *The Big Bang Theory* I watched yesterday. I just can't focus on my breathing."

Mom started petting me gently on my belly, softly moving her hand in circles. It felt so good that I felt myself falling asleep.

I watched her, and she looked so much happier.

Ten minutes later, a timer went off. I looked at her face—it kind of looked like it was lit up. From ear to ear, a huge grin appeared, and her big brown eyes twinkled. Her whole face looked softer. Finally, she looked content. "I just meditated for ten whole minutes. It was so much easier to pay attention to your fur than to focus on my breath. I never realized how soft you are." I shifted in her lap, and looked into her eyes. She asked, "Could the other meditations I've been trying to do be easier if I focused on you?"

Her smile grew even broader, "The gratitude meditation is supposed to be one of the most important practices, but it's hard to come up with something that I'm extremely grateful for every single time. I'm always grateful for you." She gave me a little kiss on my nose.

Her face looked more relaxed. It would be easier to say loving kindness phrases while focusing on you to start with than beginning with myself the traditional way. I know I have unconditional love for you." I smiled. "And, it's particularly important to stay in the moment with you when I take you for a walk."

"Pago, I think we're onto something! Meditating with your pet...Let me think about it. What if we called the meditations Petitations?" I looked at her, trying to show her the love I felt for her in my face. Little was I to know how much Petitations would shape our lives.

I'm a Schipperke. You can see that I'm absolutely adorable. When we go out, walking, some people call me a fox, some a bear, but they always smile.

I was walking down the street with Mom yesterday when a mother and young child, both with matching blond hair and blue eyes, stopped the car to get out and have a look at the pot- belly pig. How embarrassing!

Alexander was my birth name, but I go by Pago. Mom named me after Pago Pago, the capital of American Samoa. She traveled there to study the health of the native Samoans and thought it would be a cool name for a dog.

Seven years ago, when I was six months old, Mom came to a dog show where I was being shown to see if she wanted me to join her family. The judge told Dianne, my breeder, that I was a "gangly adolescent and needed to grow up." I was horrified. What if my new adoptive family overheard the judge and didn't want me?

I wanted so much to win the show to prove how valuable I was, but, oh my, I didn't even win my group.

That turned out to be my lucky day! As soon as I saw my new Mom, I felt she was the right one for me, and I just knew I'd never feel insecure again. I pulled away from Diane and did a running leap into Mom's arms. It was love at first sight—the perfect match.

I believe that things happen for a reason, and our family was meant to be. Looking back at photographs from that time, I guess the judge might have been right. My head looks like it's a little too big for my body, but I did grow into it quite nicely, if I do say so myself.

My little sister Pippi is also a Schipperke. As Mom has on her refrigerator, "Schipperkes are like potato chips. You can't have just one." She took this literally—the story of our lives.

Pippi turned three on January 21st. She can

be a nuisance, but I do love her.

Yesterday, Mom came home and let Pippi out of her crate first. Pippi jumped into mine and dragged me out by my face. Mom said it was because Pippi loves me and misses me, but I think it's just that she wants to be the boss of me. She also insists on chewing up all my toys so I can only play with them when Mom is watching.

Even so, Pippi and I have a lot of fun playing together, especially boxing in Schipperke style, standing up with our front legs in the air. We also chase each other around the living room. The first day our furniture arrived and was set in place in our new Sacramento town house, we devised an obstacle course using Mom's lavender couches and black easy chairs and, of course, the newly carpeted stairs. Just to be fair, I do give Pippi her turn to be the pursuer.

First thing in the morning is when we do most of our running around. This works out well because it leaves lots of time for Mom and me to focus on our writing in the evening while Pippi sleeps peacefully next to us.

As we chased each other around, Norman, our feline brother, watched through his bright yellow eyes from the green perch Mom put on top of the bookshelf just for him. Norman is also part of our little family. He's a grumpy gray tabby cat with a white chest, hair coming out of his ears, and long white whiskers.

He's as big as Pippi. Norman spends most of his time eating, sniffing catnip or sitting and grooming himself. From his cushion Norman can see inside the living room, up the stairs and outside to the front courtyard.

When he's content, his dark gray ears are

forward, his tail is straight in the air, and he purrs quietly. But, typically, especially when he's interacting with Pippi or me, Norman's ears are slightly back, his pupils are so constricted that you can barely see the black, his tail is curled under him, and he has a grumpy look on his face.

Although I don't like to admit it, Norman is really the boss of the house, even more so than Pippi. Norman gets to eat whenever he wants, and he sharpens his razor claws on Mom's favorite black faux leather easy chair. Mom lets him do it without even the slightest reprimand.

I'M NORMAN

Three years ago, when Norman first joined our family, Mom turned on the Pet Scan Petitation, hoping that Norman, like the rest of the family, would sit on her lap and Petitate with her. Not Norman—he just got up, rolled his eyes, twitched his striped tail and pranced out of the room. Mom frowned for a few moments before I jumped into her lap and we continued with the Petitation.

Along with playing, we spend a lot of our free time listening, as Mom reads us interesting research studies. Just the other day, she told us about the research that analyzed a combination of several studies focusing on the factors that contribute to the meditator's happiness and well-being. I love hearing about science and, if I do say so myself, I'm quite adept at learning it.

Pippi seems more interested in finding Mom's socks and chewing holes in them or playing with her "indestructible" toys, but Norman always seems to be around while Mom is reading.

How did *The Petitation Companion* come to be and why am I the one writing it?

One day, Mom was walking with her friend Stacy and Ginger, Stacy's French Bulldog. (I kind of have a crush on Ginger, but that's neither here nor there.).

Both Stacy and Ginger were suffering with terrible anxiety and were depressed after Stacy and her girlfriend broke up. Mom gave them the password so they could stream and experience the Petitations.

We met Stacy and Ginger on a walk a week later, and they were singing the praises of the program. They both found the Pet Scan and the Basic Petting Petitation especially calming and relaxing.

They reported that they slept better at night when they practiced the Petitations right before going to bed.

The thought occurred to me in one of those *ah ha* moments: Someone had to organize the stories, research, and Buddhist underpinnings into one fun book. We could call it *The Petitation Companion*. Why shouldn't I be the one to write it? I spend the most time practicing the Petitations, and listening to the discussions about the relevant research on Buddhism and meditation.

And, given that I struggle to eavesdrop on so many of Mom's conversations, both in person and on the phone, I can certainly understand humans' struggles and the impact the Petitations can have on Mom's life and the lives of the people around her. Most important of all, I love *Petitating* with Mom.

In all the chapters I will introduce you to at least one Petitation that you can stream from the website.

The Petitation Companion describes ten Petitations. Notice the lists describing the way to practice each of the Petitations. We hope you learn from the science and quasi-Buddhism and take delight in reading about our adventures.

In Memoriam

I'm Pago

ONE

The Petting Petitation

&

The Pet-Scan

Last Tuesday Pippi and I dragged Mom down the street toward the park so we could catch up with Cathy and our best friends, her pups Carson and Lilly. Both Carson and Lilly are adorable miniature poodles, as white as Pippi and I are black. They have casual cuts with short fluffy hair, just the way we like them. Mom's friend Cathy doesn't quite believe us, when we describe how meditation has been changing our lives. Even though her partner meditates, Cathy wouldn't even consider trying.

Mom needed non-meditators to beta test Petitations (As far as I could tell, this is just a fancy description for recruiting people not involved in the creation of the Petitations to test them.)

"Cathy, just give it a try." Mom pleaded. Cathy gave her one of those hand waves, the kind that Mom's Grandpa used on Nanny, when he had run out of patience, and needed to brush her off, "You know how I feel about that meditation malarkey. I don't need to meditate to relax."

Mom presented her with her most enticing grin. "How about if I take you out for a glass of wine and garlic fries at the winery you've been dying to drag me to?" That offer was too good to turn down, and Mom, striking wile the iron was hot, made arrangements for the next day.

We thought that Carson would be best suited to meditate given that his demeanor was mellower than his sister's, so he became the first guinea pig.

When Mom beta tests, she starts with the Petting Petitation, the most basic of the Petitations. I've learned from the Dharma talks that Mom plays online, that in the Buddhist tradition and in some of the secular mindfulness practices, an anchor is chosen for a simple meditation so that you focus in the present moment, rather than worrying about the future or dwelling in the past. Typically, the anchor that is chosen is the breath because it is always with you and can be relaxing for some people.

However, Mom has told me that she's not the only one who finds that the breath is a difficult anchor and that sitting and focusing on the breath for even a brief time can be frustrating and daunting.

When Carson and Cathy arrived, Pippi, always playing the alpha dog, barked, showed her teeth, and made poor Carson cower behind Cathy. The only reason that Pippi isn't a show dog and we're so lucky to have her in our family, is that she tried to boss the older dogs at her breeders' kennel, and the older dogs wouldn't have it.

Once Pippi showed Carson who was in charge for the millionth time, Carson and Cathy sank peacefully into the lavender couch with the light green pillows for their journey into the world of mindful Petitations.

Mom took out her new Apple laptop with the bright blue hard case. She fiddled with it a bit, scowling in frustration before she was able to find the Petitation she was looking for.

I glanced at Mom, "My therapist remembers quite clearly my saying it was hogwash and that I adamantly refused to participate. All I remember was that it was extremely uncomfortable, as my mind refused to quiet and kept going to places I didn't want to visit, especially in light of the amount of psychological pain I was in at the time. I was especially worried about impending grant deadlines and my failing relationship.

It took me another ten years before I was willing to give meditation a real try and then only because I was desperately unhappy." Mom looked like she was about to cry, as she talked about that time in her life.

Maybe that's why Norman doesn't like Petitating. Could there have been something difficult in his life before he came to live with us? He was a shelter cat. so it's very possible he went through some abuse that rears its ugly head when he tries to quiet his mind.

Mom paused briefly and then continued in a more upbeat tone, her face relaxing a little. "But most pet lovers can focus on stroking their pets for at least a few minutes.

This can be how the fur feels or the rhythm of their heartbeat or breathing. In the Petting Petitation, that is exactly what you do—focus on Carson." Mom looked over at Carson and Cathy and smiled.

If it's still too difficult to sit, you can count strokes.

Touch is magic for dogs. In fact, in one study, scientists found that dogs were more likely to move toward people who were giving them physical attention than verbal attention, even when the physical attention was being given to them by a stranger and the verbal attention was coming from their owner.

Then Mom added something I've never really understood "Try to be as nonjudgmental as possible." Cathy asked, "How do I refocus non-judgmentally?" I perked up. Mom looked pensive, "When I chastise myself for my wandering mind, that is judgment. We're humans and our minds are going to wander. Noticing it, labeling it, and including our pets are what the Petting Petitation is all about. And, we tend to make it even worse by passing judgment on our judging."

Mom continued, "If Bobby, the eight-month-old baby in the next apartment cries and I say to myself 'What a horrible child, why can't he be quiet so I can meditate?' I'm being judgmental.

Then when I get angry at myself for being so judgmental. I'm being very unkind to myself or, in the Buddhist world, shooting the second arrow.

The first arrow is a normal judgment—that's normal—getting upset that Bobby is interrupting my meditation.

The second arrow is judging myself for judging Bobby. If I just listen to the crying and focus on bringing my attention back to petting Pago, that's being kind to myself and makes for a better Petitation." Cathy thought about it, and a moment later she nodded and smiled.

Petitate with your pet
Share mindfulness meditation
Enhance your life
& the life of your pet
Improve all your relationships

I jumped onto my favorite seat on Mom's lap and Pippi sat next to her. Norman assumed his regular position on top of one of the TV cabinets, where Mom had put a comfortable cushion for him. Mom thinks he is open to learning about Petitations, but Pippi and I know the truth—he's taking it all in, planning to taunt us later.

Mom has become expert at stroking both Pippi and me at the same time, one with each hand. Pippi likes to be petted all down her body, while I prefer circular strokes on my belly.

We all relaxed, listening to the music that cousin Steve had composed and recorded. Mom's voice guided us to stay in the present moment by noticing when our mind wandered, gently and non-judgmentally labeling it as observing, planning, judging, remembering, or worrying and then easing our attention back to stroking us and listening to the music. We

Petitated for about eleven minutes and then Mom chimed the musical Tibetan Singing Bell.

Mom had spent about an hour trying various Tibetan Singing Bells until she found the one that was perfect for ending the recordings of the Petitations.

Mom asked Cathy what it was like for her. We all braced ourselves for a negative response, given Cathy's previous attitude that was anti-meditation.

Cathy broke out into a broad smile, "It was the longest time I've ever sat and petted Carson. The music was wonderful. It was so relaxing. I concentrated on the music and on how soft Carson's fur is." Carson was beaming with pride. Cathy's feedback was music to our ears.

My family (except Norman, of course) knows that the Petting Petitation is relaxing for us, but it's nice to hear someone else's feedback. Could we actually have converted Cathy, a hardcore anti-meditator? Maybe there's even hope that we might reach Norman.

Later I recognized that the music had changed. We were on to my favorite *Petitation*, the Pet Scan. I wagged my short tail (looked like I was just wiggling my butt to those who don't understand me well).

The other day Norman and I had an argument over the roots of the Pet Scan. He had heard on one of the Buddhist Dharma talks Mom was listening to that there was something called the body scan. (See, I told you Norman pays attention.)

I really thought Mom had created it on her own. Norman haughtily told me that the body scan that Mom used as a model for the Pet Scan became particularly well known in the Western world through the work of Jon Kabat-Zinn, a doctor who secularized meditation in the United States and started an eight-week Mindfulness Based Stress Reduction (MBSR) program way back in 1979.

Jon Kabat-Zinn introduced meditation to help his patients deal with pain when nothing else seemed to work. He started leading meditation and gentle movement therapy in the basement of the hospital, even though his colleagues thought he was a bit insane.

He began to conduct research on his methods almost immediately, and MBSR, has been shown in the scientific literature to be effective for all kinds of illnesses, both physical and emotional, including psoriasis, back pain, substance abuse, mood disorders and much more. [ii]

For a change, I appreciated Norman's input and even learned something new. In the body scan, the meditator scans her body from head to toe focusing on each part.

There are similar relaxation meditation techniques where the meditators relax various parts of their bodies. This can be done by tensing and releasing each body part, envisioning each one being filled up with warm light or by paying attention to each body part until it relaxes.

With the Pet Scan, the meditator focuses instead on the body of the pet to create a relaxing experience for both of them.

Cathy watched as Pippi lay down to play with her chew bone. Norman, still up on his perch, was concentrating on grooming his coat with his rough pink tongue.

Mom held me and Cathy held Carson in front of her, as their eyes scanned our small bodies. My fur is thick and a glossy blue-black with a ruff.

tummies, our hips, our legs, our toenails and finally our tails, as instructed by Mom's voice through the recording coming from the computer with the music in the background.

We all thoroughly enjoyed it, as they studied us with their eyes, and stroked us, including a really long time as they massaged our ears and tummies.

Mom smelled my freshly-bathed fur and newly-brushed teeth (We both love my new vanilla mint toothpaste.) and was mesmerized by my heartbeat and breathing. Cathy frowned a little when she smelled Carson's breath; perhaps he was due to have his teeth cleaned.

As Mom did the Pet Scan, she found a lump on my leg. We later went to the nice vet who helps take care of me at our animal hospital. My doctor always sits on the floor with me instead of making me sit on the cold metal table and showers me with pets and kisses. I do hate it when they have to stick me with needles to draw blood or give me shots.

I don't like needles at all! But I'm always brave, and afterwards they give me liver treats. This time they took a little bit of the lump to check for cancer.

Mom panicked because she had lost Hyjinx, her last Schipperke, to mast cell cancer. Hyjinx was Mom's first Schipperke. He must have been a hoot. Mom always talks about how he would wallow in mud with people pointing and laughing. He also loved to swim but wasn't very good at it and swam in circles, sometimes needing Mom to rescue him.

We waited two excruciatingly long days to hear from the vet. It turned out to be a benign tumor that would just go away on its own. What a relief for all of us.

Back to the Petitations...Mom gave Cathy the password to stream the Petitations so Cathy could use them with Lilly, who was struggling with anxiety problems. I really hope that the Petitations can help Lilly. Anxiety is no fun. Although I've never had an anxiety problem, I hate being scared, even for short periods of time.

On Monday, Pippi, Mom and I ran into Cathy with Lilly and Carson at the park. Of course, Mom was dying to know how they were enjoying the Petitations. Cathy enthusiastically said "Carson loves them and Lilly seems to be a bit less anxious, but that could be the Prozac she was taking. I feel even more connected with my pups, and I love Steve's music. I do sometimes fall asleep though," she admitted sheepishly. Mom grinned, "Sometimes I fall asleep too."

"There's no right or wrong way to Petitate." It's so much fun to have something to share with my friends. I asked Carson and Lilly how they liked the Petitations.

Lilly faced us. "Awesome. Both my moms are spending more time paying attention to us and they seem even calmer than they were before they started Petitating. I can't wait until more of my friends are Petitating."

WE'RE JUST PLAYING

THE PETTING PETITATION

- 🐾 Join me in finding your Petitation posture, with your pet either in your lap or right next to you. You should be comfortable, but not so comfortable that you are going to fall asleep.
- 🐾 Take three deep breaths, in through your nose and out through your mouth.
- 🐾 Scan down your body, recognizing any sensations or emotions you are feeling.
- 🐾 Choose your desired length of time and set a timer.
- 🐾 Start by petting your pet the way she likes it best.
- 🐾 You may want to change where you stroke your pet if she gets restless.

- 🐾 You can also choose to focus on your pet's breathing or heartbeat.
- 🐾 Every time your mind wanders label it as *observing, planning, remembering, judging or worrying and* then refocus on stroking your pet.
- 🐾 If your thoughts fall into more than one category label them as *both.*
- 🐾 If they fall outside these categories, label them *as none*. It's not what label you choose that matters, just as long as you label your thoughts and go back to paying attention to your pet.
- 🐾 When it is over, scan down your body again, recognizing any sensations or emotions you are feeling to assess whether the Petting Petitation impacted your body or your mood.

THE PET SCAN

- Find your Petitation posture, with your pet in your lap or right next to you.
- Take three deep breaths, in through your nose and out through your mouth.
- Start by looking at your pet overall. What color is he? Does he have any markings? Is he large or small? Is he short or tall? Is he long or short haired or even hairless?
- Smell your pet. Does he smell like his favorite shampoo or maybe he spent the day in the mud and needs a bath?
- Focus on the various parts of the body.
- Start with the ears. Are they pointy or floppy? Are they the same color inside as they are outside?

Are they soft? You may want to spend a few moments massaging the ears. Move to the top of the head. Does it feel different from the ears?

- Look into your pet's eyes. What color are they? What shape are they? Does he have funny hairy eyebrows?
- Focus on the snout or nose. Is it big or small?
- Touch the nose. Is it dry and hot or moist and cool?
- Look at the mouth. Are the teeth white? Does his breath smell like your favorite toothpaste? Or do his teeth need to be brushed?
- Travel down to the shoulders and back. Can you feel muscles, or is he bony?
- Feel the tummy. Is he thin or does

he have a pot belly? My dogs insist on a few moments of attention when rubbing their bellies.

- 🐾 Look at the legs. Does he have short or long legs? Are they bony or muscular?
- 🐾 Touch the nails or claws. Are the nails long or short? Or are your cat's claws razor sharp?
- 🐾 Finally, does he have a tail? Is it long or short? Does it stick straight out or does it curl up behind him? Is he wagging his tail or is your cat twitching his tail telling you that he wants the Pet Scan to be over?
- 🐾 How do you feel after the Pet Scan? Do you feel more connected to your pet? Does he seem more relaxed? How about you?
Is there anything you noticed during the Pet Scan that you hadn't noticed before?

TWO

The Wisdom Petitation

Mom rounded up Pippi and me. What was going on? "Guys," Mom said, "we may have to move to Sacramento." Sacramento, I thought, where the heck is that? The name sounded familiar. Oh yeah, I remembered reading the word on a tomato juice can. Doesn't she keep that in the pantry in case I get sprayed by a skunk?

I loved where we lived. Why was she taking us away? Didn't she care about *my* feelings? How would we find another great four mile walk along the bay? How would the geek (goose/duck) pond get along without us?

What about our friends? The thought of moving had me terrified.

Mom took Pippi and me with her when she went to try to find a new place for us to live. The first one was horrible. It was dirty and smelly and the paint was peeling. And, worst of all, the landlord was mean—he kept looking at me and making an ugly face.

The next one was terrible and the one after that was the worst of all.

Finally, we arrived at a townhouse complex. The unit we liked had three bedrooms upstairs. Pippi and I could run up and down all day long. That was going to be so much fun! It was demolished, but the man promised that it would be finished in time for us to move in. He really didn't want to show it to us, but Mom turned on her charm.

She batted her big brown eyes as she

pleaded, "I have to see it. We must have a home to move into. Please let us take a look. I promise I'll be very careful and I won't trip." We carefully walked on the floorboards, stepping over the tools, through the old sheet rock. The stairs could have been a problem. They hadn't even been carpeted yet.

Back downstairs I peeked out through the glass doors and saw a real backyard with a fence. Half was a concrete patio and half had loose bark. What fun! We'd always wanted a backyard. I've seen barbecues in the park.

The smells were awesome! I could just see myself begging while Mom cooked, and I knew she would give me a sample of something, just a small piece of hamburger. Pippi would dig in the bark and get it all over the place. But Mom wouldn't mind; Pippi gets away with everything.

Suddenly, a loud noise shook the whole house. Mom said it was just a train. I do like trains, but Mom asked "Would it wake us up in the middle of the night? How do you feel about the noise from the train? You looked a little nervous."

I looked into her eyes, trying to communicate to her that I wasn't scared and I thought she knew the decision she had to make. The man took us to another apartment, a different size, but it was already finished. He told us that ours would look just like it. I sat there wagging my whole body. "Please, please pick this one, I love it."

We left and Mom told the man we would be back in an hour. As soon as we got out to the sidewalk and saw all the huge trees, we were in love. We knew it was still summer so the leaves were still green.

But we were in Sacramento, not San Francisco, and we envisioned the leaves turning orange and red and yellow and brown in the fall.

We took a long walk and found a geek pond even bigger than the one near our old apartment. Mom had been so worried that she wouldn't be able to see the goslings and ducklings in the spring. Her whole face lit up and her eyes twinkled. This might have been what flipped the switch for her.

But then Mom started to look troubled. "We need to do the Wisdom Petitation." Mom knew this one by heart. We sat down on a park bench right next to the townhouse complex. We didn't even need Cousin Steve's music. All we had to do was listen to the chirping of the birds and the humming of the insects.

Mom looked directly at me, and I knew she was trying to see the decision through my eyes. "The Pros and Cons...It was perfect for us. It had an extra bedroom that Mom and I could use to do our writing—a real office.

It had two stories and only one neighbor. We could run up and down at all hours. Everything was new in the apartment. Mom would love having her own washer and dryer. No more laundry hell."

And she kept repeating how much she loved the trees and the geek pond and the yard. So many spots in the sun for me to veg out. Mom's face looked a bit less tense as her frown started to turn into a smile. The townhouse is close enough to downtown so that we can enjoy what the city has to offer.

It was if she had read my mind, "What about my friends? And your friends? How can we just pick up and leave them all to move to a place where we knew only one person?

I guess that would work itself out." Mom meets people really easily and we would be only 90 minutes from our old neighborhood.

"It really feels right, guys." Mom went back into the office and gave the man a check. I started to jump up and down because all I wanted to do was run up and down those stairs and hang out in the backyard.

I CAN BE THE BUDDHA DOG TOO

THE WISDOM PETITATION

🐾 Join me in finding your Petitation posture. This can be with your pet in your lap or next to you or, if she is unavailable or doesn't feel like Petitating, you can just close your eyes and picture her. Because of the nature of this Petitation, you may want to memorize it and have it to draw on during tough decisions.

🐾 Take three deep breaths, in through your nose and out through your mouth

🐾 Check in with your body. Do a scan from your head down to your feet, noticing any tension, sensations or emotions.

🐾 Think about a problem or dilemma that is troubling you and bring to mind a wise pet.

- 🐾 Talk through the pros and cons with the pet.
- 🐾 Think about what the pet would tell you throughout the process.
- 🐾 Once you have weighed the pros and cons, try to make a decision.
- 🐾 Pay special attention to how this feels in your body. If you feel more relaxed, like a weight is taken off your chest, it is likely this is the best decision you can make at the moment.
- 🐾 If you feel increasingly tense, then you may want to gather more data or revisit the Wisdom Petitation later.

Petitate with your pet
Share mindfulness meditation
Enhance your life
& the life of your pet
Improve all your relationships

THREE

The Walking Petitation

Pippi and I love the Walking Petitation. Mom says it's especially helpful when she's dealing with frustrating situations.

One afternoon, Mom frowned, and her shoulders went up so high, they looked like they would touch her ears. She was on the phone with Joan, a Buddhist Dharma teacher, who Mom was working with to put one of her meditation classes online. "I know we want to have video, but you're working on a PC and I'm working on a Mac. I'm not sure we're going to find compatible software. I'll keep investigating."

She ended her call and sighed. "Pago, I love this project and plan to help meditation practitioners put their teachings on line, but I have a love-hate relationship with the current technology."

Mom exhaled deeply and frowned. She got up and started walking slowly across our spacious living room with its high wooden ceilings. She labored over each step. "Heel, toe, heel toe, breathe deeply," she muttered under her breath.

This is what Buddhists call a walking meditation. I watched while Mom did this for another five long minutes. (Do you have any idea what five minutes feels like when you're just watching and waiting?)

Pippi played with her red super indestructible Kong, one of two toys that she hasn't been able to tear apart. The other Pippi-safe toys are made from the material that's used to make fire hoses. All my soft, squishy stuffed animals, the rabbits and teddy bears and puppies, have been put away because Pippi chews their stuffing out.

Just recently Mom has started putting them in my crate with me, where Pippi can't get them. It's only when I got my old friends back that I realized how much I had missed them, especially the gray squirrel and the mallard.

"Pago," Mom spewed, "This is just not working. The walking meditation is supposed to be relaxing, but I'm just feeling more and more tense. I've always felt like a failure because I've never found the walking meditation particularly helpful." Her eyes did brighten slightly as she decided to give up on the walking meditation and called us to her.

I gleefully jumped up and down, reaching heights of around five feet, something that we Schipperkes are known for, when I saw Mom reach for her walking clothes. She donned her black sweat pants and a light gray sweat shirt with the UC Berkeley Bear on it, and her favorite pair of grey running sneakers with the hot pink trim.

Mom took out our gear—bright green for me and purple for Pippi. She put on our matching collars along with the harnesses, so I knew that this would be a longer walk, not just a quick one for us to do our business. She played the Walking Petitation on her computer before heading out for our walk.

Even Mom needs a reminder before going out: pay attention to your surroundings and be in the present moment.

Against the background of Cousin Steve's music, Mom reminded us with her voice emanating from the computer that we must leave all technology behind and really pay attention to what's going on around us. This means looking at the sky, the trees and the flowers in the park, the stars, the moon, and the planets at night, and smelling everything: nature and the stores and restaurants as we pass by them.

The bars are my favorite part of the walk. I love the smell of stale beer and the dark, inviting environment where everyone can be anonymous. But Mom told me in no uncertain terms that I am too young for bars and that we won't drink, even when I get older.

Mom suggests that we socialize, but Pippi and

get jealous and Pippi barks, and even tries to nip.

Not me, I silently wallow in self-pity.

The recording guides the listener to pay particular attention to what the dog is noticing and smelling. She said to try to experience the walk from the dog's perspective.

Mom did suggest that if you can't completely put your concerns out of your mind, you should give yourself a time limit, and then spend the rest of the time in the present moment. She usually recommends no more than 15 minutes to worry or think.

practice mindfulness meditation with your pets

Mom, Pippi, and I left the house with the best intentions. Mom wanted to get out of her own head. But she wasn't paying attention to the present moment. Her shoulders and jaw were still tight, and she was looking down at the dirt path directly in front of her. She didn't even look at her favorite, almost full-grown goslings at the geek (*goose/duck*) pond.

They were starting to look like their parents, but not quite as large. Her "teenagers," she usually calls them. She also failed to take in the trees surrounding the pond and the children playing in the playground. And, worst of all, she wasn't even looking down at Pippi and me with that smile of adoration that she usually presents to us during the Walking Petitation.

I had an argument with Norman just last week when I told him how important it is to walk dogs. I explained:

> In a study conducted in four cities, scientists found that five times as many dog owners reported meeting someone in their neighborhood whom they didn't know before they moved in, when compared to non-dog owners. Even owners with indoor pets such as cats or rabbits were more likely to make social connections. Half of pet owners received informational support, advice and instrumental support from people they met through their pets. [iv]

Norman started grooming himself, pretending not to pay attention, but he likes a good study as much as I do. So, I continued,

> It's not just socialization that having pets improves. Just getting our families off their butts to play with us can reduce their illness and chance of early death. Scientists found that walking for 20 minutes a day can lengthen life and decrease chance of an early death by 16-30% depending on other factors.[v]

Another research team conducted a meta-analysis and found that sedentary behavior was associated with higher rates of all-cause mortality, cardiovascular disease, cancer mortality, cancer incidence and type II diabetes incidence.[vi]

I could sense that I was losing Norman so I tried to make it more relevant to his life,

Even taking time to walk around and play with cats and dogs while watching TV can help promote health. Studies show that a sedentary lifestyle is dangerous . [vii] [viii]

City walks are fun (This is in Legoland)

Norman couldn't deny that exercise is helpful for mood which is good for our entire household:

Studies have shown that physical activity has been associated with decreased symptoms of distress, including depression, anxiety, and panic disorders.[ix,x,xi]

Perhaps more significant to the self-centered part of me, walking is not only good for humans, but it's also good for us dogs.

Pippi and I are less likely to get into trouble and suffer from health issues because of our daily walks. And Pippi definitely calms down better at night when she's had a day filled with activity. Not me, though, I'm a great sleeper and pretty mellow, no matter what.

Dog experts proclaim that when we dogs get our daily dose of exercise, we are less likely to engage in excessive barking, chewing, digging, and other behaviors that our families find troublesome (although sometimes we do these things just because they are fun).

Exercising can help keep us agile and limber, reduce digestive problems and constipation, help the timid or fearful build confidence and trust, help those of us that are hyper at night sleep better, and help keep weight under control [xii][xiii]

I do digress but I love scientific research...

Back to our Walking Petitation... Finally, we passed a bulldog, and Mom decided to get out of her own head and engage with the world. She usually talks with everyone we meet, even when she's preoccupied.

She looked up, stopped walking and started chatting with someone new. He was about 5'8", tan, stocky, with hazel eyes and silver hair, and said his name was Bill and his bulldog was Harley. As Mom spoke with Bill, she finally cracked a smile.

Harley looked me up and down with that ridiculous expression that bulldogs always seem to have, given their under bite and dumb-looking bulging eyes.

I presented my best smile and we sniffed each other's butts. I gave a little bark of approval. Mom gave Harley a pat on the head and gave Bill a card with information on Petitations. Looking at Bill, she said. "I'm trying to get feedback on the Petitations right now. All it takes is about an hour of listening to meditations you share with your pet or that center on your pet and give me some honest feedback."

"If you're willing to do this with me, I'll give you the Petitations to stream for free."

They set a time on Friday afternoon for us to go to Harley's house. I was psyched. I gave Harley one more quick bark goodbye.

I hoped that this uplift was not temporary and would last the rest of the walk, but Mom's smile disappeared and she looked down at the now dark paved path in front of us. She needs so much interaction to improve her mood. I wish that walking with Pippi and me were enough for her.

At last, Mom looked around. We sat on our favorite bench overlooking the rose garden, with its red, white, lavender, fuchsia, yellow, peach, and pink roses, and enticing fragrances. I sat on Mom's lap and Pippi sat next to us.

Mom's jaw finally unclenched, and her eyes brightened. Her shoulders relaxed and she breathed deeply. We remained there for about ten minutes and then moved on to the streets of Sacramento.

First, we all noticed the enticing smells emanating from the bakery. I begged, looking straight at Mom with my saddest puppy dog eyes.... but and I knew the answer before it was obvious.....nothing for any of us there.

Because of the anti-dog laws, dogs are only welcomed in outdoor seating. If it's just Mom, Pippi and I, we must sit outside.

We finally reached our favorite restaurant. It's very inviting with trees in planters, wooden tables, chairs, benches, and big umbrellas in red, yellow, bright pink, orange, aqua, blue, almost as many colors as we saw in the rose garden. They even have water dishes outside for us.

I love the smell of the beer that spilled on the ground and both Pippi and I started licking it, until Mom moved us to another table. She filled the water bowl with the outside hose that the restaurant provided just for us and ordered her favorite chopped salad with blue cheese dressing—no onions, along with unsweetened iced tea.

She ate slowly, and Pippi barked at only one of the dogs.

We left the restaurant and headed for home, but then we encountered a funny looking little tan pup with big round eyes. Pippi growled at her. Mom got annoyed. "Pippi" she yelled pulling back on her leash. "I'm so sorry," Mom told the Chihuahua's heavyset owner with the blonde ponytail and dark blue eyes.

Mom's forehead wrinkled and her mouth turned down. "Pippi, why do you always have to embarrass me?" Pippi and I exchanged annoyed glances—we both hate tiny, yappy dogs. It always infuriates us when Mom blames us every time we bark, especially when it's the other dog that starts it.

We continued our walk in the shade of the trees with the unique houses on both sides of the broad streets. Mom slowed down, loosened her grip on Pippi and looked at us with a twinkle in her eyes. She picked me up and gave me a big hug.

"Pago, I think I'm ready to figure out the next steps on my project. I shouldn't be surprised that the Walking Petitation grounds me. I created it," she laughed.

Music to my ears!

When we got back to the house, Mom took out her video camera. She set it on a tripod so that she could record herself talking in front of the cream-colored wall in the dining room.

She turned it on and sat on the wooden dining room chair. "Testing one, two....is this going to work? Testing one, two, testing one, two." She played it back and grinned. "Yup, Pago, I think this is our answer. The sound quality is great and it synchs perfectly.

Sometimes you just have to go back to basics. Some technology is just not quite there yet."

While Mom was preoccupied with the video camera, Pippi had a mischievous smile on her face. She looked toward the bathroom. The door was opened and we could see inside as we approached it, that there was a roll of toilet paper partially unfurled and beckoning us.

I gave Mom a quick glance. She was still *futzing* with the video camera. I looked back at Mom one more time and crept slowly toward the bathroom, trying to imitate Norman's cat walk, the sneaky one he does so well. There was almost a full roll. I gripped one corner of the end with my teeth and ran out the door, down the hall to the bedroom, around the bed and down the stairs, with the toilet paper trailing after me. Pippi took up the chase, getting in on the action.

After festooning the stairs and the entire bedroom with white squares, I jumped on the bed to chew on a piece. Pippi retraced her steps, went back into the bathroom and pulled the cardboard toilet paper roll off the new silver stand. She chased it for a while, batting it with her paws and then brought it on the bed to tear it up. I prefer the toilet paper, but Pippi thinks the cardboard core is more fun.

Pippi and I looked at each other, feeling just a little guilty, our heads cocked as we looked at the mess. Oh no, what now?

We Live for our dogs.

THE WALKING PETITATION

- 🐾 With this Petitation, join me in listening to the Petitation first, and then proceed to go out on your walk with your dog.
- 🐾 Bring technology along only for emergencies. Here the goal is to focus on your dog, not your iPod or your phone.
- 🐾 If you have something that you feel you absolutely must think or worry about, allow yourself a period to spend thinking about it. I usually recommend no longer than 15 minutes. It's easier if you set a timer.
- 🐾 Observe your surroundings as you take your walk: the smells, the sounds, the colors, the shapes, the temperature, the wind, the sun, or perhaps even the rain.

- Stop and look at the trees, flowers, grass, skyline, bodies of water, restaurants and stores during the day or the moon, and stars at night.
- Notice the smells and the feel of the sun and the wind. React to and pay attention to other dog walkers and those who are paying special attention to your dog.
- Ask about breeds or strike up a conversation.
- If your pets are friendly, allow them to be petted by the people around you.
- Try to see things from your dog's perspective. Allow him to sniff and give other dogs "pee- mail."
- Give your dog as much attention as possible throughout the walk. What is most important is that you relax and enjoy the moment.

FOUR

The Equanimity Petitation

After we returned from the Walking Petitation, Mom was trying out her video camera for a project as we accomplished our toilet paper disaster in the bedroom. She walked in and saw Pippi on the bed gnawing on the cardboard core and me tearing up the toilet paper.

In the past, Mom would have lost it. Her face would have turned the same shade of fuchsia as the roses in the park, as she yelled at us, stomping around and trying to pick up the pieces of soggy toilet paper, and then, finally, she would lock us in our crates. We don't really mind our large dog crates with our blankets when *we* choose to inhabit them.

But we hate when Mom uses them to punish us and locks the doors. It's so humiliating. We're basically good pups, but we do have some slip-ups, very minor ones.

Why does she keep leaving the door to the bathroom open again and again? She knows we can't help ourselves. You'd think she would stop setting us up for mischief.

Norman was peering from his lofty perch with his eyes gleaming and a smirk on his face. "You guys are going to get it." He loves to see us get in trouble.

But, then again, Mom's been reciting the mantras for the Equanimity Petitation almost every night. Perhaps she might be able to use her newfound balance and see the humor in the situation. The room did look kind of funny with white toilet paper plastered all over.

If the kids can decorate their homes so they look so humorous when we go trick or treating, why can't we decorate our bedroom? Holding my breath, I sat in the middle of the bed, and waited for Mom to enter the room.

Mom approached the doorway and looked at the mess we had made. She frowned and made a really ugly face. Then she caught herself and sighed. She chanted, almost inaudibly, "They are who they are...It is as it is...Pippi and Pago are who they are..." She looked around the room, and then at Pippi, who, with the remnants of a toilet paper roll in her mouth, was giving Mom her unique sideways glance. (Even I think she looks cute when she does that.) Mom couldn't help but let out a small chuckle as she cleaned up the room.

"Looks like you guys had a party. I guess that proves I should pay more attention and close the bathroom door" Mom's change in attitude had been gradual as she practiced the Equanimity Petitation regularly.

The whole point of the Equanimity Petitation is to give the Moms and Dads the time and space to calm them down and allow for an appropriate response that is not driven by reactivity or just emotions. Not to say that your pets don't need to be reprimanded when things go awry, but you don't want to say inappropriate things or, even worse, strike out at your pets and hurt them physically. You don't have to like what your pet has done, just accept it.

A few more seconds of the Equanimity Petitation mantra allows for this space.

Ever since Mom added the Equanimity Petitation to her regular practice, she has been more patient with us and has moved more quickly from anger to acceptance.

Another way to think of the Equanimity Petitation is cultivating balance in all areas of your life. The idea is that if you are able to accept things as they are, then you won't find yourself reacting to negatives or stressors as intensely as they come your way.

So how exactly can you develop equanimity? One way is to practice other Petitations, such as the Petting Petitation and the Pet Scan, to develop basic mindfulness. You can also, for this Petitation, relax your body from head to toe, one part at time, trying to establish a balance. This allows you to be in the present moment without reacting to everything that is occurring around you.

There is also an Equanimity Petitation that is specifically focused on developing balance. First, you imagine a time when you have felt this balance or equanimity with your pet. Notice how it feels in your body. Then say the mantras: "Things are as they are. May I accept things just as they are." Notice whether there are any more changes in your body.

Next, think of a time when things haven't been so balanced, say the mantras, and see if it effects changes in your body. Perhaps your dogs or cats ate something they weren't supposed to eat. Maybe the cat peed outside his litter box.

Maybe your dog chewed on and destroyed the fifth Bluetooth (Something I have to say, I love to do.). Observe the effect saying the mantras has on your body.

Then, perhaps most difficult for many of us, say the mantras for yourself:

"I am as I am. Things for me are as they are."

Spend some time feeling this in your body. You end the Equanimity Petitation by refocusing on the peaceful time you felt with your pet at the beginning of the Petitation.

Practicing the Equanimity Petitation can be helpful to establish equanimity overall, and by stating the mantras, to help allow you the space to react appropriately when you are in a tough spot.

THE EQUANIMITY PETITATION

- Join me in finding your Petitation posture. This can be with your pet in your lap or next to you. If she is unavailable or doesn't feel like Petitating, you can just close your eyes and picture her.
- Take three deep breaths, in through your nose and out through your mouth.
- Scan down your body, recognizing any sensations or emotions you are feeling.
- Picture a time when you felt particularly peaceful with your pet. Spend a few moments really feeling this in your body. Do you feel relaxed? Do you feel spacious? Do you find yourself smiling?

- Repeat the following mantras:
  "Things are as they are.
   May I accept things just as they are.
   My pet is who she is."
- Think of a time when you have had difficulty with your pet. Sit with this for a few moments noticing how it feels in your body.
- Do you feel tightness in your back, neck, face or shoulders? Do you feel a knot in your stomach?
- Say the mantras:
  "Things are as they are.
  May I accept things just as they are.
  My pet is who she is."

  Notice how this feels in your body. Is there any relief?
- Now there is a little self-equanimity. Say the mantras:
  "Things are as they are.
  I am who I am.
  May I accept myself just as I am."

- 🐾 Notice how this feels in your body.
- 🐾 Finally go back to imaging the peace you felt with your pet in the beginning and say the mantras:

    "Things are as they are.
    May I accept things just as they are.
    My pet is who he is."
- 🐾 Scan your body again, recognizing any sensations or emotions you are feeling.
- 🐾 Remember to practice these mantras so that they are very familiar when you most need to access them to minimize damaging reactions due to emotional responses.

FIVE

The Loving Kindness Petitation

Schipperkes are often adopted into the same families as horses because we are particularly good around them. That's why Mom adopted Hyjinx, her first Schipperke. At the time she had Magdalena, a beautiful Peruvian Paso with a long black mane, forelock, and tail.

I only knew Magdelena for a short while, but there are pictures of her all over our house. You can't even imagine the excitement I felt when I found out that I was going to a ranch with Mom to observe equine therapy. As we pulled up near the barn, I could smell horses in the air. There were eight horses all together.

They were much bigger than Magdelena and didn't live in stalls like she did. Rather, they hung out in a huge paddock.

On our first day, the therapist introduced all the horses and told us about their personalities and their roles in the herd. Wyakin was the horse that they called their "special needs horse."

Mom asked the therapist what they meant. I moved forward to eavesdrop.

"When he was born, they didn't think he was going to make it past a few days. He has lived a healthy lifestyle, but he's a bit anti-social. They even have difficulty putting a harness on him."

After meeting all the horses, the therapist asked Mom to choose a horse that she felt connected with.

Of course, she chose Wyakin. She petted Wyakin, looked into his cocoa brown eyes and told him how special he was and that she would come every other week and bring an apple especially for him.

He seemed a little nervous, pacing back and forth on his muscular legs. She recited the mantras from the Loving Kindness Petitation to show him how much she accepted him just the way he was.

"May you be happy. May you find peace. May you be healthy. May you live a life of ease. May you find unconditional love."

She tried to put a halter on him, but he backed off and ran away. Over the next couple of months, she worked with Wyakin, always saying the Loving Kindness Petitation and trying to show him her unconditional love. It took several months. But as she worked with him, he became more and more trusting. He leaned into her when she stroked him, and he even stood up to the dominant mare so that he could have Mom's undivided attention.

In another situation, Mom needed the Loving Kindness Petitation. Andrea, one of Mom's friends, had to visit her sick mother and leave a dog she had just adopted from the local animal shelter with Mom. He turned out to be a really difficult dog. He chewed on the furniture, scratched at the door and ran away when she tried to attach his leash.

Mom quietly repeated the Loving Kindness Mantras, "May you be happy. May you find peace. May you be healthy. May you live a life of ease. May you find unconditional love."

As the days went by, the dog moved closer and closer to her when she turned on the Loving Kindness Petitation. He was able to feel her acceptance and love. Eventually, he settled down. He acted less tense, more relaxed and he stopped chewing up everything in his path.

The Loving Kindness Petitation also includes a focus on a difficult person in your life. Mom had a friend named Jillian who expected her to come to her rescue all the time. Jillian lived two hours away from our new home in Sacramento.

One night, Jillian was especially needy and wanted Mom to be with her, but Mom had just returned from a trip to the East Bay and couldn't make the drive again, especially late at night.

I overheard Jillian's side of the conversation from my favorite eavesdropping position: "Then you just aren't a real friend. I need you and you just aren't here." This was a trigger for Mom—like most people, she likes to be considered a good friend. Her face and jaw tightened. She looked like she was ready to cry from pure frustration, but she didn't give in.

Instead of remaining in her angry state, she included Jillian in a Loving Kindness Petitation. She chanted, 'May you be happy. May you be peaceful. May you live a life of ease. May you be physically and emotionally healthy. May you have unconditional love." Mom's face gradually relaxed... she sighed.

For many humans, having loving kindness toward themselves is even more difficult than having loving kindness for other people who make their lives difficult.

How many times have you beaten yourself up and reprimanded or criticized yourself in a way you would never do, even to your worst enemy? The Loving Kindness Petitation commences with saying the Loving Kindness mantras for yourself:

"May I be happy.

May I be at peace.

May I be physically and emotionally healthy.

May I have a life of ease.

May I experience unconditional love."

With time, this can help you attain the self-love you deserve. Sometimes I wonder if all this Loving Kindness really makes a difference. We just need to look at two powerful studies:

Dr. Fredrickson and her colleagues assigned half their sample to a loving kindness intervention group and half to a wait list control. Within nine weeks, those participating in a loving kindness practice (similar to the Loving Kindness Petitation but focused solely on humans) showed increases in experiences of positive emotions including love, joy, gratitude, contentment, hope, pride, interest, amusement and awe.

Over time they were linked with mindful attention, self-acceptance, positive relationships with others, and physical health. They also had lower symptoms of depression, a higher life satisfaction.[xiv]

Another study by Hutcherson and colleagues showed that the brief lovingness meditation can increase social connectedness with strangers.[xv]

So, the Loving Kindness Petitation not only can help you feel good, but it may be helping you emotionally and physically. As with all the Petitations, there are no negative side effects.

THE LOVING KINDNESS PETITATION

- ❀ Join me in finding your Petitation posture. This can be with your pet in your lap or next to you, or if she is unavailable or doesn't feel like Petitating, you can just close your eyes and picture her.
- ❀ Take three deep breaths, in through your nose and out through your mouth.
- ❀ Scan down your body, recognizing any sensations or emotions you are feeling.
- ❀ Look at your pet or close your eyes and picture your pet.
- ❀ Say the following mantras: "May you be happy. May you be peaceful. May you live a life of ease. May you be physically and emotionally healthy. May you have unconditional love."
- ❀ Notice how this affects your body

- Think about someone you love deeply.
- Picture this person and say the mantras:
  "May you be happy. May you be peaceful. May you live a life of ease. May you be physically and emotionally healthy. May you have unconditional love."
- Notice how this affects your body.
- Picture a human or a pet you are having difficulties with.
- Say the mantras:
  "May you be happy. May you be peaceful. May you live a life of ease. May you be physically and emotionally healthy. May you have unconditional love."
- Notice how this feels in your body.
- Now you are going to do perhaps the most difficult loving kindness,

to yourself:

"May I be happy. May I be peaceful. May I live a life of ease. May I be physically and emotionally healthy. May I have unconditional love. May I be kind to myself."

🐾 Once again, picture the pet you began with and repeat the mantras.

🐾 Scan down your body, recognizing any sensations or emotions you are feeling.

SIX

The Self Compassion Petitation

Sometimes we all beat ourselves up and take ourselves for granted, even me. Yesterday, I was super focused on how adorable everyone always thinks Pippi is.

Pippi has the almond shaped lighter brown eyes that I always think of as preferable in a Schipperke. And Mom is thrilled that Pippi always seems to want to take care of everyone. When someone is hurting, she gets this concerned look on her face. Her eyes slant, and she cocks her head as she licks the spot of the injury. I have to admit, she does make people feel better, and she's awfully cute.

Then there's Norman. All he has to do is purr to make people feel better, something that just comes naturally. Humans never tire of petting his soft grey and white fur and listening to his purring.

He doesn't know how lucky he is. Although I can make Mom feel better by encouraging her to exercise and licking the tears as they stream from her eyes, I just can't fix her the way Norman can.

Norman had just proudly spit out the research at me yesterday:

We cats purr at the perfect MHz to heal ourselves and humans. And, we cure ourselves. Scientists did a research study where they studied cats that had fallen from an average of five stories and, although some got hurt, 90 percent lived. This would be impossible for dogs. [xvi]

He put his paw up on the side of his face and looked very arrogant, as he continued: *Compared to cats, dogs don't recover from illnesses as quickly, and they have illnesses like arthritis and cancer more often.*[xvii]

I was feeling down on myself yesterday and decided to do a reverse Petitation. This time, I would do the Petitation for myself instead of letting the human do the Petitating. I've heard the Compassionate Petitation so many times, I know it by heart.

First, I had to choose what I was going to focus on. That was easy: feeling bad about not being able to make people feel better immediately, like Pippi and Norman. Then I created a safe space in my mind. I chose the duck and goose pond in McKinley Park. The mallards and the beautiful striped female ducks were quacking, some swam, others sunned.

A little girl with curly red hair was feeding the geese, while her proud Mama looked on. I wondered what it would feel like to pat her on her head like people petted me. How would it make her feel? Just going there in my mind helped me to relax a little.

In my mind I invited Beth, Mom's meditation teacher, who was one of the kindest and wisest people we ever knew, to join us at the pond. Beth was a homeopath, so I thought she'd understand the importance of all kinds of helping. I pictured Beth coming over, and I sat comfortably in her lap for a few moments, relishing her presence.

Beth started, "People all contribute in their own way. The way Pippi contributes is important: she makes people feel better. The way that Norman gives to others is through his purring, relaxing them when he sits in their laps." Beth looked at me with her big, kind, brown eyes.

We sat for a moment. Then, in her always compassionate and gentle voice she said, "Pago, you contribute in so many ways. First, it's just by being you, by loving your family. You spread joy and happiness wherever you go. How many people and dogs stop to talk to you and smile when you go out walking each day?" I reflected for a minute. She was right. We are constantly having positive interactions.

I looked right into her eyes, again, smiling, and shifted in her lap.

"And don't forget about the Petitations. You were the reason that they were created in the first place and you are writing The Petitation Companion. What you are doing, putting yourself and your ideas out there is a very brave and difficult thing to do. People have already started practicing the Petitations and they have definitely had an impact on your friends, relatives and family." I grinned at Beth. "Writing with your Mom has strengthened your bond and, given your recent move to Sacramento, she really needs you right now." Hmmm. I never thought of it that way. I always forget how tough writing is, especially because on most days I love it and it definitely is my passion, especially writing about Petitating. Next, it was my turn to share my thoughts with Beth. "Thank you so much. Sometimes it's so easy to get lost in what I can't do instead of what I can do and how I do help people and other animals." I sighed and couldn't help but frown. "I really miss you!"

Beth died of cancer a year ago. She was way too young. I could have stayed in Beth's lap in my mind's eye all day, but it was time for the Petitation to end. She gave me one more kiss on my nose and was gone.

I took a few more moments to feel her in my heart. Then I opened my eyes. I know that whenever I need her, Beth will be there.

The Compassionate Friend Petitation was first created for humans to practice with their pets— just like Beth was my compassionate friend.

It starts the same way. First, you come up with a safe and comfortable place in your mind's eye. It could be in nature, perhaps on a beach or in the woods, where you can listen to the music of the surf or the song of the wildlife, or you could choose to be in a room with a fireplace or a warm bath. Visualize the twinkling candles and the fragrances surrounding you.

You then decide on a pet, living or deceased, to help tell you what you need to hear. It's best to have your pet near you, but if you can't, then having her in your mind's eye is fine. This pet has to feel wise, compassionate and non-judgmental, as most of us are. Try to listen to what your pet is saying to you. If nothing comes to mind then that's fine too. But usually, there is something to hear.

Enjoy your pet's company for a few more minutes, then take some deep breaths and open your eyes. Remember, your pet is there for you whenever you need her, full of wisdom and compassion and completely non- judgmental.

OUR "GEEK" POND

THE COMPASSIONATE PETITATION

- ❧ Join me in finding your Petitation posture. This time you don't need to have your pet nearby.
- ❧ Take three deep breaths, in through the nose, out through the mouth.
- ❧ Scan down your body, recognizing any sensations or emotions you are feeling.
- ❧ Picture in your mind's eye a peaceful and safe place. This can be indoors or outside—by a fireplace, or a waterfall, or the ocean...
- ❧ Welcome, in your imagination or in real life, your non-judgmental, accepting, loving pet coming to join you.
- ❧ Sit for a moment with your pet and feel his warmth and love.

- Talk to her about something that is troubling you. If nothing is troubling you, that's fine too. Just enjoy her company.
- Listen carefully to her response if you've spoken to her.
- Take some time to absorb her loving feedback, noticing how this feels in your body.
- Spend a few more moments with her.
- Thank her and take some deep breaths.
- Scan down your body, recognizing any sensations or emotions you are feeling.
- You can welcome back your compassionate friend at any time.

> *This was adapted from the work of Kristin Neff, with permission*

SEVEN

The Appreciative Joy Petitation

Mom heard the loud ring tone, the Mexican Hat Dance. It sounded pretty silly to me, a shiny black furry Northern Californian, but she explained to me so many times that she chose it because it was one of the tunes in her father's repertoire of songs that he whistled. Mom said her Dad even taught it to his parrots, so when Mom talks to her mother, she hears it over and over in the background—how annoying!

I'll never understand living with parrots, but, then again, I can bark and yelp and whine and be generally obnoxious also. Mom picked up the large smart phone with the black rubber case.

I'm not sure she knew that I was the eavesdropping canine, but I heard her: "I'm happy for her, but I just can't help feeling jealous of Dianne's new job. There's nothing worse than feeling this knot in my stomach when I know I should be a good friend and share her joy."

Mom's face was tight, her jaw clenched and she was furrowing her brows. Something must have her really upset. Aunt Jaimie's calm voice on the other end was loud enough for me to overhear. After about five minutes of griping, Jaimie convinced Mom to turn on the Appreciative Joy Petitation.

Mom sighed deeply. "Ok, ok...let's do it." She booted up the computer, complaining the whole time about how long it was taking, while staring at the flying owls with big eyes on the blue tapestry across the room.

Beth, Mom's first meditation teacher, had taught her about how owls protect us. Beth's way too early death had knocked us all off our perches and is a constant reminder that we must enjoy life and stay in the present moment. Beth would have loved the Petitations, especially the Appreciative Joy Petitation.

I watched Mom as she forced herself to breathe deeply and saw that her worry lines relaxed a little. Rummaging around the computer files in iTunes she found the Appreciative Joy Petitation. Mom's cousin Steve had just composed the music and sent it to her. Steve's music was sweet and calming with lots of flutes and piano, yet not so mellow that it put us to sleep. We're so lucky that cousin Steve is in our lives. His wonderful music has greatly enhanced the Petitations.

Sometimes, we just sit together and listen to the music without even practicing the Petitations. Jumping up into Mom's lap, I had mixed feelings. Life is a dialectic. I felt sorry that Mom was in so much pain, but, what the heck...she has a job...working with her friend to put her meditation class on line.

It's puzzling that Mom is still envious of her friends locked into traditional jobs. She can be such a brat. She gets to spend way more time with me when she works from home.

I was relieved when I heard the music for the Appreciative Joy Petitation and looked forward to some relaxing time. Sometimes the tension gets to be too much.

With a puzzled look on his face, Norman, who seems to be getting more and more curious about Petitations, gruffly asked, "What's this one about?" I smiled, happy to have sparked his interest—I'm always seeking Petitation recruits.

Mudita, or the Ancient Buddhist Appreciative Joy meditation, has been practiced to enhance happiness by accepting and feeling joy in the success and good fortune of others. By enhancing joy for others, you diminish envy and jealousy, the opposites of appreciative joy. It's not like there isn't enough joy to go around. Envy and jealousy make all of us feel bad and cultivate hatred."

Mom and Jaimie did the Appreciative Joy Petitation for the full ten minutes. Mom's voice came from the speakers in the computer, "First, think of your pet when you have enjoyed her the most. It could be when she first arrived as a puppy or kitten, when she graduated from advanced obedience or won agility training, or when he sat purring in your lap."

"How does this feel in your body?" Mom's voice from the computer continued, "Does it make you start to smile? Does your stomach feel like it's relaxing? What about the muscles in your face?" She continued, "In order to cultivate this even further, say, May you be happy, joyous and free...May this feeling of joy continue and continue. May it never end." Mom's face began to look more relaxed and the corners of her mouth started to turn up into a small smile.

Next is the difficult, yet critical part. Picture before you, the being who is experiencing joy, but who is evoking jealousy or envy in you.

Repeat the mantras:

"May you be happy joyous and free

May your joy continue and continue."

Really try to feel it authentically and deeply. Take some deep breaths. How does this feel in your body?"

She finished with, "Being happy for another being cultivates your joy. If you could feel joy for all of those who are happy, imagine how much happiness you would hold in your heart." Mom broke into a full smile. Her shoulders came down and her face and jaw were much more relaxed.

What a relief. I too felt more relaxed. I guess there is enough time for Norman, Pippi and me to Petitate with Mom and enough room in her heart for all of us. And I know, being the oldest and her writing partner, that I will always be special to her.

Sometimes it's so hard with Mom. She can be impossibly stubborn. She created the Petitations, yet she can hesitate to use them. I should learn how to use the computer so, instead of barking or whining, I could just turn on the appropriate Petitation and do it all by myself. I can do everything else.

THE APPRECIATIVE JOY PETITATION

- 🐾 Join me in finding your Petitation posture. This can be with your pet in your lap or next to you, or if she is unavailable or doesn't feel like Petitating, you can just close your eyes and picture her.
- 🐾 Take three deep breaths, in through your nose and out through your mouth.
- 🐾 Check in with your body. Do a scan from your head down to your feet noticing any tensions, sensations or emotions.
- 🐾 Think about a time when you have been especially happy to have your pet in your life.
- 🐾 Soak in this joy and peacefulness in your body.
- 🐾 Now picture someone who you have felt envious or jealousy toward in some way, big or small, to cultivate it even further.

- Say the mantras:

  "May you be happy, joyous and free...May this feeling of joy continue and continue. May it never end."

- Take some time to let it soak into your body. Try to feel it authentically.

- Ponder the fact that their happiness is in no way diminishing your joy. There is enough happiness to go around. In fact, if you feel joy for this person, you will most likely communicate this to the person consciously or subconsciously.

- Scan your body for physical sensations and emotions. Notice how the Petitation has changed the way you feel in your body. If you still feel the envy, take a break and repeat the Petitation.

EIGHT

The Grief Petitation

Wolfie was my best friend. He was shiny and black just like me, but he had yellow eyes. I guess I should have figured out that he wasn't a dog like me, because dogs don't have yellow eyes, but that didn't matter to us. He and I used to wrestle and play. We played most of the time, and when it was time to rest, we cuddled together.

When Wolfie died from cancer, I couldn't figure out what was wrong with me. I was sad all the time and I didn't even want to eat. I had always been hungry and I didn't understand why my food just didn't taste very good any more.

I heard Mom complaining to the vet that I had stopped eating, and they were talking about something called *depression*. I couldn't figure it out. All I knew was that I was sad and angry and felt tired, and I wasn't even hungry. Wolfie was my best friend and I couldn't find him. He was gone. I was lonely. I had no one to play with.

Mom looked as sad as I felt. I heard her talking about what she had learned from research: that it's important when someone dies to hold both the grief and positive memories in our hearts and minds at the same time, so we both did the Grief Petitation as we tried to get through our grief. I didn't really understand all of this, but I knew it made me feel just a little bit better every time we sat in her room and did the Petitation together.

Mom told me the Grief Petitation was created to help us through this terrible experience. First, we remembered what Wolfie, our beautiful cat, added to our lives. Mom explained through the computer "Remember the way your dog welcomed you by running around in circles when you first came home, the way your cat purred or rubbed against your legs. It could be how your horse leaned into you as you brushed her." You are guided to feel these positive feelings in your body. Maybe there is some relaxation, a slight smile on your lips, a feeling of a growing heart or expansiveness. When Mom explained how it could help, I thought I should be feeling better. When I think about how Wolfie slept with me, cuddling with Mom, it warms my heart. Or, how we used to run after each other—so much friendly teasing, but so much fun.

Next, Mom explained, you are guided to get in touch with and validate your difficult emotions. When I think about how Wolfie died too early from cancer, I get sad and angry. My body tightens and my stomach feels like it has a knot in it. I stare for a long time at the beautiful picture of Wolfie or a mosaic that Mom created to look like his face, trying to remember him as much as I can, while still allowing myself to feel the grief.

Finally, as Mom directed, I allowed myself to be guided to get back in touch with the positive memories. In this way I validated my difficult feelings and held onto the positive feelings at the same time. This helped stop us from going into a deep depression.

Mom says that if the humans feel themselves slipping into a serious depression, they should, along with practicing the Grief Petitation, seek professional help—either a support group or an individual counselor.

I'm trying very hard to feel better and, on some days, when Pippi and I are having fun, the sun is shining, and the birds outside are happily chirping, I do feel better. Wolfie won't be back, but just knowing him made our lives better.

WE MISS YOU, DEAR MIKEY

HELPING TO GRIEVE

THE GRIEF PETITATION

- 🐾 Join me in finding your Petitation posture. If it is a pet that is failing then you may want to have him on your lap or next to you. Otherwise, you may want to have a picture of him nearby.
- 🐾 Take three deep breaths, in through your nose and out through your mouth.
- 🐾 Pay attention to your body. Do a scan from your head down to your feet noticing any tension, sensations or emotions.
- 🐾 Think about a time when you have been especially happy to have your pet in your life.
- 🐾 Try, if possible, to soak in this joy and peace in your body. Notice how this feels.
- 🐾 Allow yourself some time to grieve.

- Return to remembering the positive times you had with your pet. Look at the picture of him or pay attention to him in your lap or next to you.
- Go back and forth as often as you want for as long as you want. Remember, losing a pet is the hardest part of being devoted to beings that live such short lives, but not holding on to the positive aspects can lead to serious depression.
- If you think it may help, seek a counselor or a pet grief support group.

NINE

The Gratitude Petitation

It's so hard for me to understand humans. We dogs are so much more grateful. As a species they have it made. Mom has a warm shower, toilets inside the house, a car, a smart phone, a shiny new laptop, and she gets to choose a different outfit each day. Perhaps, most important, is that she decides what she wants to eat, when, and how much. These are just a few things to appreciate.

Unlike humans (or cats, for that matter) who are sporadically grateful, we dogs appreciate almost everything. When Mom and Aunt Lisa came to the door today, Pippi and I jumped up and down and ran around in circles, while Pippi sounded her ear-piercing bark, acting like she hadn't seen them in years. It doesn't really matter whether it's been ten minutes or a long weekend.

Then again, when Mom walked through the door to our apartment several times today, her face lit up, as to be fair, it does more often than not. Then she broke into a huge smile, let us out of our corral, picked us up one at a time, and gave us big hugs. She called us her "little angels."

She means it from the bottom of heart. She's showing us extreme gratitude each and every time. But even this level of gratitude doesn't match the ecstatic appreciation that we dogs feel throughout the day.

Each time Mom picked us up as she came through the door, Norman stared at us with a condescending look. His eyes narrowed as he lifted his paw up to the side of his cheek. I've talked to him about how he should, like humans, develop a gratitude practice. He didn't quite understand what was so important about a "gratitude practice".

I thought that Brene Brown, a renowned social science researcher informed by interviews with hundreds of participants and personal experiences could best help me express to Norman the importance of gratitude.

"When it comes to gratitude, the word that jumped out at me throughout this research process is practice. For years, I subscribed to the notion of an 'attitude of gratitude.' I've since learned that an attitude is an orientation or a way of thinking and that 'having an attitude' doesn't always translate to a behavior.

For example, it would be reasonable to say that I have a yoga attitude. The ideals and beliefs that guide my life are very in line with the ideas and beliefs that I associate with yoga. I value mindfulness, breathing, and the body-mind-spirit connection. I even have yoga outfits. "But, *let me assure you, you, my yoga attitude and outfits don't mean jack if you put me on a yoga mat and ask me to stand on my head or strike a pose. Where it really matters—on the mat—my yoga attitude doesn't count for much"*[xviii]

Norman walked away with a short meow, holding his grey and white tail high. I jumped in to continue to emphasize my side of the argument. This time I talked about more research from one of the best-known scientists on gratitude, with hopes of convincing him. I pulled out information from the Greater Good Science Center Library.

Robert Emmons researched over 1000 participants, ages 8-80, and found that gratitude practices improved physical, social and emotional health. These practices can be simple. Keep gratitude journals where you remind yourself of the gifts, grace, benefits, and good things you enjoy. Set aside time on a daily basis to recall moments of gratitude associated with ordinary events, your personal attributes, or valued people in your life who give you the potential to interweave a sustainable life theme of gratefulness.[xix]

The Gratitude Petitation definitely fits these parameters. Norman looked into my eyes, and it took a few minutes before he looked away. Although he didn't appear to be completely convinced, at least he seemed to be listening.

Yesterday, Mom really needed to practice the Gratitude Petitation. After greeting us, her expression quickly changed to a weak smile and furrowed brows. She sat down on the sofa, cuddled under the multi-colored blanket embroidered with the big Schipperke in the almost-unpacked living room and tears started streaming down her face.

"Pago, I am feeling so much lonelier than I thought I would. It seems to come and go, but today has been really hard."

I jumped into her lap and licked her salty tears. Sometimes it's frustrating to be a dog. I wanted to tell her everything was going to be OK and that it would be helpful to take us out for a walk to an outdoor brunch place, or even better, to turn on the Gratitude Petitation.

She started to pat my belly and kiss my forehead. Her tears stopped, her face relaxed, and the corners of her mouth turned up slightly. She got up, and it seemed like she had read my mind, as the music from the Gratitude Petitation emanated from her computer.

Norman slowly and quietly slunk into the room when he heard the music and saw that Pippi had jumped into Mom's lap. He meowed softly. Usually he just sits on his perch guarding the room whenever we Petitate, but this time his face softened.

Pippi said, "Shush, Norman. We're practicing our Gratitude Petitation. Hear Mom's voice coming from the computer? She's guiding us to focus first on me and how wonderful I am. Of course, given my dozens of positive attributes, this is easy." Pippi changed her position slightly,

"Mom has been encouraging us to notice how it feels in our bodies. I really enjoy when she focuses on me. She gives me extra pats and it feels great". Pippi smiled. "She then focuses on another being that brings her gratitude. I bet it's Pago this time. Or maybe, it's even you."

Norman started to smile before he caught himself. Next, Mom asked us to pay attention to the various parts of our body that make us feel grateful. Most humans are not thrilled with every part of their bodies. "Not I," Pippi bragged, "I find myself particularly beautiful in every way." Then Mom refocused her attention on Pippi. While she is guided to pay attention to the changes in her own body, as she is experiencing gratitude, sometimes she finds it difficult to do it for herself.

When the Petitation ended, Pippi jumped down and suggested to Norman that he try it. Norman scowled, but he did jump into Mom's lap. Although Norman is negative and stubborn, he's also very curious, and I could tell that the science I had cited had an impact on him.

Mom's smile got even wider and her eyes brightened. She went through the whole Petitation again, this time petting Norman as he purred loudly. She tried not to make a big deal of it so that Norman wouldn't be put off, but, wow, was I excited. This was the first time that Norman actually Petitated!

THE GRATITUDE PETITATION

- 🐾 Join me in finding your Petitation posture. This can be with your pet in your lap or next to you or if she is unavailable or doesn't feel like Petitating, you can just close your eyes and picture her.
- 🐾 Take three deep breaths. Breathe in through the nose and out through the mouth.
- 🐾 Scan down your body, recognizing any sensations or emotions you are feeling.
- 🐾 Think about how grateful you are to have your pet in your life.
- 🐾 Take a few moments and focus on how this feels in your body. Perhaps you feel a little more relaxed in your jaw, shoulders, back or belly. Or maybe you feel lighter or more

expansive. If not, that's certainly normal, just notice what you are feeling.

- Next expand this circle to include another important being in your life for a few moments. Check back into your body.
- Expand the circle to include yourself —the various parts of your body you are grateful for (your lungs, your heart, your legs, your hands, your brain). If your body doesn't work the way you would like, focus on the ways in which it does work. Check back into your body.
- Perhaps most difficult, think about pets you have lost and the gratitude that you have for the time you had with them.
- Finally, go back to the pets you started focusing the Petitation on, those that are still with you.

🐾 Scan down your body, recognizing any sensations or emotions you are feeling and how they have changed since the beginning of the Petitation.

I can Petitate with your children

TEN

Too Close to Our Hearts

I walked into the kitchen with Pippi and overheard Mom talking to her mother. She was crying, not just tearing up, I mean really crying HARD! Big tears were rolling down her face.

"Not Daddy, he's the smartest, kindest, funniest man in the world." And now the doctor (And we all know he's not a chauvinist because he sees a lady doctor.) told him he had to make an appointment with a cardiologist THIS week. It seemed he had some irregularities, that she called AFIB, or flutters, or something like that. She was saying something about all kinds of life changes and medication and who only knew what else

—I doubt that Mom even heard much of it, she was so upset.

Mom's Dad was 77 years old, but still working full time, didn't intend to quit, could do anything and everything, and never ever got sick. He and her Mom were married for 52 years and, you know what, they still held hands, all the time. Pretty funny. You only see that in movies on late night TV.

Mom immediately went to her computer to see if there was any evidence of meditation helping with AFIB. It didn't take her very long to find several articles and studies showing that meditation could have positive effects on the heart.

Mom continued into the phone, Shouldn't we turn Daddy into a Petitator? We know he loves his dogs almost as much as he loves Mom, and he should be able to pick one that would sit on his lap. Wesley is a full-time lapdog. In fact, he doesn't even care whose lap he's sitting on. So, he would love to Petitate."

Willie, Grandpa and Grandma's Tibetan Spaniel might also work, but only if he's in the mood. Look at the expression on his face. Do you really think he would cooperate with anyone? "Tibbies," as they are called by everyone who loves them, have minds of their own. He doesn't look cooperative like me, the geeky Buddha dog or even Norman. (No, let's leave Norman out of this. He's off the chart.)

So, Grandpa does have choices. I overheard, or do we call it eavesdropped, when Mom was discussing the situation with Grandma.

First, we had to convince Grandpa to try Petitating. "That was easy," Grandma said, "I just won't feed him until he's finished." We all know it won't take very long.

Cousin Steve's music is so pleasing that it alone will sell it to him. (And Cousin Steve is Grandpa's nephew, the one who everyone always said most resembles him.)

"Did Daddy Petitate?" Mom asked Grandma later that first day. By the look on Mom's face, I could tell the answer. Mom was smiling and laughing and clapping her hands as Grandma told her that Grandpa really did like the Petitations.

Grandpa said to Mom, "Elisabeth, I love these. How did you learn to do this? It was so relaxing, and it helped me to feel less stressed."

Now I know Grandpa will be just fine. He has the best heart in the whole world and when he practices the mindfulness meditation with his dogs and Petitates regularly, he surely will be able to continue with his wonderful life.

PETITATION TIPS

🐾 As you learn to Petitate you may want to start small. Begin with short Petitations and build your Petitation muscle. You wouldn't go to the gym expecting to lift hundreds of pounds right away.
The more frequently you Petitate, the easier it will be to develop your Petitation practice.

🐾 As you Petitate, you will most likely notice that your thoughts jump around much like a monkey swings from branch to branch. This is often called having a "monkey mind" (gotta love those animal metaphors). Just be gentle with yourself and bring your attention back to the Petitation.

🐾 If your pet is uncomfortable or wants to get away, either switch to another Petitation where she doesn't need to be with you or take a break and try again at another time.

🐾 We pets also need to develop a Petitation practice. You want your Petitation posture to be comfortable but not so comfortable that you fall asleep(unless that's your purpose, in which case, by all means, lie down). Mom and I often Petitate sitting up in bed.

- At the beginning and end of each Petitation, I recommend that you do a body scan. Pay attention to physical sensations (tension, cold, heat, tingling, sounds) and your emotions. This helps you to identify how the Petitation is affecting you and how you change over time. Try to vary the Petitations. You want to develop various parts of your brain.

- There is no wrong way to Petitate. Just try to stay focused so that you are not worrying about the past or the future.

- You may want to set an intention with each Petitation and your Petitation practice as a whole.

- Are you trying to calm your mind? Do you want a better connection with your pet? Are you trying to relieve anxiety? Remember, Petitate to have fun.

- Get more out of your meditation practice and enjoy your time with your pet.

REVIEW OF PETITATION PRACTICES

THE PETTING PETITATION

- Join me in finding your Petitation posture, with your pet either in your lap or right next to you. You should be comfortable, but not so comfortable that you are going to fall asleep.
- Take three deep breaths, in through your nose and out through your mouth.
- Scan down your body, recognizing any sensations or emotions you are feeling. Choose your desired length of time and set a timer.
- Start by petting your pet the way she likes it best. You may want to change where you stroke your pet if she gets restless.
- Every time your mind wanders label it as *observing, planning, remembering, judging* or *worrying* and then refocus on stroking your pet.

- If your thoughts fall into more than one category label them as both. If they fall outside these categories, label them as none. It's not what label you choose that matters, just if you label your thoughts and go back to paying attention to your pet.
- When it is over, scan down your body again, recognizing any sensations or emotions you are feeling to assess whether the Petting Petitation impacted your body or your mood.

To receive the free Petitations and music, go to www.mindfulpetitations.org. Click on the page labeled "for book owners" and use the following password:

Page149PC

THE PET SCAN

- Find your Petitation posture, with your pet in your lap or right next to you.
- Take three breaths, in through your nose and out through your mouth.
- Start by looking at your pet overall. What color is he? Does he have any markings? Is he large or small? Is he short or tall? Does he have long fur or hair, short fur or hair or is he hairless?
- Smell your pet. Does he smell like his favorite shampoo or maybe he spent the day in the mud and needs a bath?
- Focus on the various parts of the body.
- Start with the ears. Are they pointy or are they floppy? Are they the same color inside as they are outside? Are they soft? You may want to spend a few moments massaging his ears.
- Move to the top of the head. Does it feel different from the ears?
- Look into your pet's eyes. What color are they? What shape are they? Does he have funny hairy eyebrows?

- Focus on the snout or nose. Is it big or small? Touch the nose. Is it dry and hot or moist and cold?

- Look at the mouth. Are the teeth white? Does his breath smell like your favorite toothpaste? Or does he need a tooth brushing or a trip to the dentist?

- Travel down to the shoulders and back. Can you feel muscles or is he bony?

- Feel the tummy. Is he thin or does he have a pot belly? My dogs insist on a few moments of attention when rubbing their belly. Look at the legs. Does he have short or long legs? Are they bony or muscular?

- Touch the nails or claws? Are your dog's nails long or short? Or are your cat's claws razor sharp?

- Finally, does he have a tail? Is it long or short? Does it stick straight out or does it curl up behind him? Is he wagging his tail or is your cat twitching his tail telling you that he wants the Pet Scan to be over?

- 🐾 How do you feel after the Pet Scan? Do you feel more connected to your pet? Does he seem more relaxed? How about you?
- 🐾 Is there anything you noticed during the Pet Scan that you hadn't noticed before?

THE WISDOM PETITATION

- Join me in finding your Petitation posture. This can be with your pet in your lap or next to you or, if she is unavailable or doesn't feel like Petitating, you can just close your eyes and picture her. Because of the nature of this Petitation, you may want to memorize it and have it to draw on during tough decisions.
- Take three deep breaths, in through your nose and out through your mouth.
- Check in with your body. Do a scan from your head down to your feet, noticing any tension, sensations or emotions.
- Think about a problem or dilemma you are struggling with.
- Recall a wise pet.
- Talk through the pros and cons with the pet. Think about what the pet would tell you throughout the process. Once you have weighed the pros and cons, try to decide.
- Pay special attention to how this feels in your body.

- 🐾 If you feel more relaxed, like a weight is taken off your chest, it is likely this is the best decision you can make now.
- 🐾 If you feel increasingly tense, then you may want to gather more data or revisit the Wisdom Petitation later.

THE WALKING PETITATION

- With this Petitation, join me in listening to the Petitation first and then proceed to go out on your walk with your dog.
- Bring technology along for emergencies only. The goal here is to focus on your dog, not your iPod or your phone.
- If you have something that you feel you absolutely need to think or worry about, allow yourself an allotted amount of time to spend thinking about it. I usually recommend no longer than 15 minutes. I recommend that you set a timer.
- Notice your surroundings as you go on your walk: the smells, the sounds, the colors, the shapes, the temperature, the wind, the sun, or maybe even the rain.
- Stop and look at the trees, flowers, grass, skyline, bodies of water, restaurants and stores during the day and the moon, stars at night. Also notice the smells and the feel of the sun and the winds.

- 🐾 Smile at and pay attention to other dog walkers and those that are giving special attention to your dog.
- 🐾 Ask about breeds or strike up a conversation. If your pets are friendly, allow them to be petted by the people around you.
- 🐾 Try to see things from your dog's perspective. Allow him to sniff and give other dogs "pee-mail".
- 🐾 Give your dog as much attention as possible throughout the walk.
- 🐾 What is most important is that you relax and enjoy the moment.

THE EQUANIMITY PETITATION

- Join me in finding your Petitation posture. This can be with your pet in your lap or next to you. If she is unavailable or doesn't feel like Petitating, you can just close your eyes and picture her.
- Take three deep breaths, in through your nose and out through your mouth.
- Scan down your body, recognizing any sensations or emotions you are feeling.
- Picture a time when you felt particularly peaceful with your pet. Spend a few moments really feeling this in your body. Do you feel relaxed? Do you feel spacious? Do you find yourself smiling?
- Repeat the following mantras, "Things are as they are. May I accept things just as they are. My pet is who she is."
- Think of a time when you have had difficulty with your pet. Sit with this for a few moments noticing how it feels in your body.

- Do you feel tightness in your back, neck, face or shoulders? Do you feel a knot in your stomach?
- Say the mantras, "Things are as they are. May I accept things just as they are. My pet is who she is."
- Notice how this feels in your body. Is there any relief?
- Now for a little self-equanimity. Say the mantras:

  "Things are as they are. I am who I am. May I accept myself just as I am."

  Notice how this feels in your body.
- Finally go back to imaging the peace you felt with your pet in the beginning and say the mantras,

  "Things are as they are. May I accept things just as they are. My pet is who he is."
- Scan down your body again, recognizing any sensations or emotions you are feeling.
- It's important to practice these mantras so that they are very familiar when you most need to access them--to minimize an over-reaction due to an emotional response.

THE LOVING KINDNESS PETITATION

- Join me in finding your Petitation posture.

  This can be with your pet in your lap or next to you, or if she is unavailable or doesn't feel like Petitating, you can just close your eyes and picture her.

- Take three deep breaths, in through your nose and out through your mouth.

- Scan down your body, recognizing any sensations or emotions you are feeling.

- Look at your pet or close your eyes and picture your pet.

- Say the following mantras:

  "May you be happy. May you be peaceful. May you live a life of ease. May you be physically and emotionally healthy. May you have unconditional love."

- Notice how this affects your body.

- Think about someone you love a lot. Picture this person and say the mantras:

  "May you be happy. May you be peaceful. May you live a life of ease. May you be physically and emotionally healthy. May you have unconditional love."

- 🐾 Notice how this affects your body.
- 🐾 Picture a human or a pet you are having difficulties with. Say the mantras:

  "May you be happy. May you be peaceful. May you live a life of ease. May you be physically and emotionally healthy. May you have unconditional love."
- 🐾 Notice how this feels in your body.
- 🐾 Now you are going to do perhaps the most difficult loving kindness, to yourself:

  "May I be happy. May I be peaceful. May I live a life of ease. May I be physically and emotionally healthy. May I have unconditional love. May I be kind to myself."
- 🐾 Once again picture the pet you began with and repeat the mantras.
- 🐾 Scan down your body, recognizing any sensations or emotions you are feeling.

THE SELF COMPASSION PETITATION

- Join me in finding your Petitation posture. This time you don't need to have your pet nearby.
- Take three deep breaths, in through the nose, out through the mouth.
- Scan down your body, recognizing any sensations or emotions you are feeling.
- Picture, in your mind's eye, a peaceful and safe place. This can be indoors or outside—by a fireplace, or a waterfall, or the ocean... Welcome, in your mind's eye, or in real life your nonjudgmental, accepting, loving pet to come and join you.
- Sit for a moment with this pet and feel his warmth and love.
- Talk to her about something that is troubling you. If nothing is troubling you, that's fine too. Just enjoy her company.
- Listen carefully to her response if you've spoken to her.

- 🐾 Take some time to really absorb her loving feedback, noticing how this has felt in your body.
- 🐾 Spend a few more moments with her.
- 🐾 Thank her and take some deep breaths.
- 🐾 Scan down your body, recognizing any sensations or emotions you are feeling.
- 🐾 You can welcome her back at any time when you need a compassionate friend.

> This Petitation is based on the work of Kristen Neff with permission.

THE APPRECIATIVE JOY PETITATION

- Join me in finding your Petitation posture. This can be with your pet in your lap or next to you, or if she is unavailable or doesn't feel like Petitating, you can just close your eyes and picture her.
- Take three deep breaths, in through your nose and out through your mouth.
- Check in with your body. Do a scan from your head down to your feet noticing any tensions, sensations or emotions.
- Think about a time when you have been especially happy to have your pet in your life. Soak in this joy and peacefulness in your body.
- To cultivate it even further, say the following mantras:

    "May I be happy, joyous and free...May this feeling of joy continue and continue. May it never end."
- Now picture someone who you have felt envious or jealous toward in some way, big or small.

- Say the mantras:

    "May you be happy, joyous and free. May this feeling of joy continue and continue. May it never end."

- Take some time to let it soak into your body. Try to feel it authentically.

- Ponder the fact that their happiness is in no way diminishing your joy. There is enough happiness to go around. In fact, if you feel joy for this person, you will most likely communicate this to the person consciously or subconsciously.

- Scan your body for physical sensations and emotions

- Notice how the Petitation has changed the way you feel in your body.

- If you still feel the envy, take a break and repeat the Petitation.

THE GRIEF PETITATION

- Join me in finding your Petitation posture. If it is a pet that is ailing then you may want to have him on your lap or next to you. Otherwise, you may want to have a picture of him nearby.
- Take three deep breaths, in through your nose and out through your mouth.
- Pay attention to your body. Do a scan from your head down to your feet noticing any tension, sensations or emotions.
- Think about a time when you were especially happy to have your pet in your life.
- Try, if possible, to soak in this joy and peacefulness in your body.
- Notice how this feels in your body.
- Allow yourself some time to grieve. Really let yourself feel the sorrow and pain. Let the tears come if they are on the surface. Validate these feelings for yourself. You may even want to do this with someone else who loved your pet or cares about you.

- 🐾 Take some time to let it soak into your body.
- 🐾 Return to remembering the positive times you've had with your pet. Look at the picture of him or pay attention to him in your lap or next to you.
- 🐾 Go back and forth as often as you choose for as long as you think it will help.
- 🐾 Remember, losing a pet is the hardest part of having beings in our families that live such short lives, but not holding onto the positive aspects can lead to serious depression.
- 🐾 It may help to seek a counselor or a pet grief support group.

THE GRATITUDE PETITATION

- Join me in finding your Petitation posture. This can be with your pet in your lap or next to you or, if she is unavailable or doesn't feel like Petitating, you can just close your eyes and picture her.
- Take three deep breaths. Breathe in through the nose and out through the mouth.
- Scan down your body, recognizing any sensations or emotions you are feeling.
- Think about how grateful you are to have your pet in your life.
- Take a few moments and focus on how this feels in your body. Perhaps you feel a little more relaxed in the jaw, shoulders, back or belly. Or maybe you feel lighter or more expansive. If not, that's certainly normal, just notice what you are feeling.
- Next expand this circle to include another important being in your life for a few moments.
- Check back into your body.

- Expand the circle to include yourself—the various parts of your body you are grateful for (your lungs, your heart, your legs, your hands, your brain). If your body doesn't work the way you would like, focus on the ways in which it does work.
- Check back into your body.
- Perhaps most difficult, think about pets you have lost and the gratitude that you have for the time that they did have with you.
- Finally, go back to the pets you started focusing the Petitation on, those that are still with you. Notice how this feels.
- Scan down your body, recognizing any sensations or emotions you are feeling and how they have changed since the beginning of the Petitation.

Endnotes

[i] Feuerbacher, EN & Wynne CD (2015). Shut up and pet me! Domestic dogs (Canis lupus familiaris) prefer petting to vocal praise in concurrent and single-alternative choice procedures. *Behavioral Processes*, 110, 47-59.

[ii] Kabat-Zinn, Jon (2013). Full Catastrophic Living (Revised Edition). Bantam

[iii] Nagasawa, M (2015). Oxytocin-Gaze Positive Loop and the Coevolutionn of Human-Dog Bonds. *Science,* 348 (6232), 333-336

[iv] Wood L et al. (2015) The Pet Factor - Companion Animals as a Conduit for Getting to

Know People, Friendship Formation and Social Support. *PLoS ONE* 10(4).

[v] Ekeland U et al. 2015. Physical activity and all-cause mortality across levels of overall and abdominal adiposity in European men and women: the European Prospective Investigation into Cancer and Nutrition Study (EPIC). *American Journal of Clinical Nutrition*.

[vi] Biswas, A et al. 2015. Sedentary time and its association with risk for disease incidence, mortality, and hospitalization in adults: a systematic review and meta-analysis. *Annals of Internal Medicine*, 162(2)

[vii] https://www.washingtonpost.com/apps/g/page/national/the-health-hazards-of-sitting/750/

[viii] http://www.mayoclinic.org/healthy-lifestyle/adult-health/expert-answers/sitting/faq-20058005

[ix] Paluska, S. A. and Schwenk, T. L. 2000. Physical activity and mental health. *Sports Medicine* 29: 167-180. Penedo, F. J. and Dahn, J. R. 2005. Exercise and well-being: A review of mental and physical health benefits associated with physical activity. *Current Opinion in Psychiatry* 18: 189-193.

[x] Goodwin, R. D. 2003. Association between physical activity and mental disorders

among adults in the United States. *Preventive Medicine* 36: 698–703

[xi] Galper, D. I., Trivedi, M. H., Barlow, C. E., Dunn, A. L. and Kampert, J. B. 2006. Inverse association between physical inactivity and mental health in men and women. *Medicine & Science in Sports & Exercise* 38: 173- 178.

[xii] Get Healthy, Get a Dog: The Health Benefits of Canine Companionship. A Harvard Medical School Special Health Report

[xiii] ASPCA—American Society for the Prevention of Cruelty to Animals, Exercise for Dogs... https://www.aspca.org/pet-care/virtual-pet-behaviorist/dog-behavior/exercise-dogs

[xiv] http://www.ncbi.nlm.nih.gov/pmc/articles/PMC3156028/

[xv] http://www.ncbi.nlm.nih.gov/pubmed/18837623

[xvi] http://veterinarycalendar.dvm360.com/why-do-pets-do-eating-grass-purring-yawning-and-catnip-reactions-proceedings

[xvii] http://www.spiritofmaat.com/archive/oct3/mthaler.htm

[xviii] Brene Brown, The Gifts of Imperfection: Let Go of Who You Think You Are Supposed to Be and Embrace Who You Are, 2010 Hazelden page 78-79

[xix] http;//greatergood.berkeley.edu/article/item/why gratitude_is_good

173

Made in the USA
Coppell, TX
13 December 2019